SERMON OUTLINES
ON
Holiness
Volume 1

BEACON SERMON OUTLINE SERIES

SERMON OUTLINES
ON
Holiness
Volume 1

Beacon Hill Press of Kansas City
Kansas City, Missouri

Copyright 2002
by Beacon Hill Press of Kansas City

ISBN 083-411-9870

Printed in the
United States of America

Cover Design: Paul Franitza

Library of Congress Cataloging-in-Publication Data
Sermon outlines on holiness.
    p. cm. — (Beacon sermon outline series)
  ISBN 0-8341-1987-0 (v. 1)
    1. Holiness—Biblical teaching—Sermons—Outlines, syllabi, etc. 2. Holiness—Christianity—Sermons—Outlines, syllabi, etc. 3. Bible—Sermons—Outlines, syllabi, etc. I. Series.
  BS680.H54 S47 2002
  234'.8—dc21

                                                    2002007692

10 9 8 7 6 5 4 3 2 1

Contents

Introduction

God's call to all His followers is to be holy as He is holy (see 1 Pet. 1:16). The highest challenge of every believer is to respond to that call through full consecration and to experience the cleansing, empowering work of the mighty Spirit of Holiness. The entire pursuit of the holy way opens new possibilities of growth and development in Christlikeness.

Every pastor bears the awe-inspiring challenge to convey God's call to holy living to his or her congregants. Christian holiness challenges believers to live at a God-designed, God-empowered level.

These sermon outlines were compiled from *Breaking Free from Sin's Grip.* In this book Dr. Frank Moore defines and interprets Christian holiness for today's generation.

Add research, meditation, and prayer to these outlines, and ask God to bring those hearing your preaching to new levels of faith and holiness.

God Had a Dream

Genesis 1:26

Introduction

As parents we all have a dream for our children. We want the best for them. We want them to become all they can be. We dream of their successes, accomplishments, and spiritual development. So God had a dream for the man and woman He created and placed in the Garden of Eden.

I. Created in His Image (See Gen. 1:27)

Our lives and relationships are like God in many ways, so we can learn more about Him and the way He wants to relate to us as He reveals himself and His incredible plan for us in a variety of ways.

1. Creation
2. Historical events
3. Personal circumstances
4. The life and ministry of Christ
5. The Bible
6. Psychological, emotional, and social makeup

II. Created on Purpose

A. We are not an accident of nature; God directly created us for personal fellowship with Him and each other, which means we possess many characteristics of His own image.

1. Self-awareness
2. Imagination
3. Complex language
4. Self-direction
5. Ability to think philosophically
6. Ability to think creativity
7. Capacity for memories.

B. God envisioned an incredible parental plan and brought it into being, and no doubt that brought Him a sense of enjoyment, a sense of fulfillment, and a Father's joy.

III. Created to Be Holy (See Lev. 11:44; 1 Pet. 1:15-16)

A. God reminds us throughout His Word that He is holy and that His hopes and dreams are for us also to be holy.

B. As a parent God has our best interest in mind and wants us to find fulfillment in daily living, but He knows the only way for His plan to work in our lives is for us to participate in His plan for our holiness.

IV. Created for Him

God created us to live our lives with Him at the center of our existence.

1. If we choose to place anything else at the center of our existence, the pieces of the puzzle will never fit together properly because God made us for himself and placed an empty spot at the center of our being that only He can fill.

2. Without Him in the center spot of our lives, life never makes sense.

Conclusion

God had a dream and created humanity in His image for the purpose of having fellowship with Him. To have fellowship with a holy God we must be holy. We are made for Him. When we leave God out of our lives, we become spiritually, emotionally, and psychologically crippled and deformed, alienating ourselves from our created purpose. God had a dream. Then God said, "Let us make man in our image, in our likeness" (Gen. 1:26).

God's Limitation

Genesis 2:16-17

Introduction

When we think of God, we think of Him as all-powerful. We think He can do anything anytime He wants to. God flung a million stars in the sky. They fell into place, and they shine just as He planned. He created planets beyond our wildest imagination and set them in motion in galaxies that reach beyond our loftiest thoughts and strongest telescopes. They rotate and interact with one another just as He planned.

I. How Did God Limit Himself? (v. 16)

A. God crafted humanity with a very different quality from the rest of His creation.

   1. He gave us life, movement, and a purpose as He did the rest of creation.

   2. But He also gave us a very powerful tool for both good and evil. We call it free will.

B. God knew our free will came with a risk. We could freely choose to love Him and obey Him, or we could freely choose to reject Him and break His heart.

   1. God took that risk because the reward of genuine love and obedience was so great.

   2. God took His hands away and hoped we would choose to walk in a morally straight line.

II. How Did God Test Humankind? (vv. 16-17)

A. How humankind met the test is recorded in 3:1-13: Free will was exercised; God's word was disobeyed; blame was passed.

B. Given the option of self-sovereignty or surrender of self-preference to the Creator's will, we chose self-sovereignty.

C. With that choice came the knowledge of good and evil and an awareness of disobeying God. Innocence was gone; we freely rejected God.

D. This choice created a change in the hearts of Adam and Eve and in the hearts of all their future children.

III. The Test Results (3:7)

A. With their choice came moral knowledge of right and wrong.
   1. They were awakened to their disobedience.
   2. Divine fellowship ended.

B. Innocence vanished in the shadow of selfish choice; with innocence went holiness. Deprived of God's presence, the human heart became depraved.

C. Little has changed in the human heart.
   1. We are still born with a bent toward self-preference.
   2. We are still deprived of God's immediate presence.
   3. We still have depraved hearts.
   4. We are still spiritually needy.

Conclusion

Read today's newspaper. Read story after story of parents abusing children, of children killing children, of lying and stealing, of murders and mass killings, of drugs and gang crimes. It is heartbreaking. It is the result of humankind's free choice. Only choosing God's will and plan can change it.

Who Is God?

Isaiah 6:3

Introduction

Who is this holy God, our Creator? We ought to learn all we can about Him, since we are created in His image. As we learn about Him, we learn more about His plans for us.

I. God Is Holiness (Ps. 99:9)

A. Holiness is not simply one positive God quality among many; it defines all of God's other attributes or characteristics.

1. Holiness defines God the way light defines the sun.
2. Holiness is the essence of who God is.

B. From His holiness flow all of God's other attributes.

II. God Is Righteousness (50:6)

A. When we say God is righteous, we mean He follows the moral rules He established. He always does the right thing.

B. So God's holiness guarantees righteous actions.

III. God Is Love (1 John 4:16)

A. A great chasm separates holiness from everything inferior. But God's love closes the abyss between His holiness and our unholiness and draws us to His loving heart.

B. He reached out to us before we even knew we needed Him.

1. He held out hope to change our unholiness into holiness.
2. So He offers us this holy gift.

IV. God Is Grace and Mercy (Eph. 2:8)

A. God's grace and mercy flow from His holiness.

B. His holiness gives us what we do not deserve (grace) and does not give us what we do deserve (judgment).

C. He shows compassion on us in our unholy spiritual condition, and He acts kindly toward us when we deserve judgment.

V. God Is Truth (John 14:6)

Truth flows from God's holiness, so we can rely on what He says to be correct.

1. He never lies, misrepresents, or misleads us.
2. So when His Word tells us that God loves us or is gracious and merciful to us, we know these statements are factual.
3. Because God is holy, He always bears truth.

Conclusion

Our God is a holy God. Holiness threads its way through all of God's other attributes to help define them. Who He is exemplifies what He wants us to be.

God's Holiness in the Bible

Leviticus 11:44

Introduction

Throughout the Bible we find numerous references to God's holiness. We can begin with Genesis and continue through Revelation.

I. The Book of Genesis

Genesis does not speak specifically about God's holiness but hints at it in various ways.

1. Unholiness always hides from holiness (see 3:8).
2. Noah pleased God because he was righteous and blameless (see 6:9).
3. God called Abram to be blameless (see 17:1).
4. Jacob encountered God's presence at Bethel as he found himself on holy ground (see 28:16-17).

II. Hearing Holiness in Exodus

A. We began to hear specifically about holiness when Moses stood before the burning bush (see Exod. 3:5).

B. After the crossing of the Red Sea, Moses sang of God's holiness (see 15:11).

III. Understanding God's Holiness

A. Our understanding of God's holiness takes shape as we read Leviticus.

1. The holiness of God and His hopes and dreams for our holiness set the backdrop of the entire book.
2. All of the symbols and images point toward holiness in one way or another (see 11:44-45).

B. The holiness code in Leviticus (see 20:26; 21:8, 15, 23; 22:9, 16, 32).

      1. This code constantly reminds the Hebrew people that wherever they go and whatever they do, they must never forget one thing—God is holy.

      2. Our call to holiness in Leviticus stems from God's holiness.

IV. Expressing God's Holiness

A. The Book of Psalms frequently references the holiness of God.

B. Everything related to God becomes holy.

      1. Holy hill (see 3:4).

      2. Holy Temple (see 5:7, 11:4).

      3. Holy heaven (see 20:6).

      4. Holy place (see 28:2).

      5. Holy mountain (see 43:3).

      6. Psalms links God's holiness and His name in praise (see 30:4; 99:3, 5, 9).

V. The Complete Picture of God's Holiness

A. One of the most complete pictures of the holiness of God comes from the life of the prophet Isaiah (see Isa. 6:1-8).

B. Isaiah's experience gives us a clear image of our holy God.

C. Isaiah's divine encounter transformed him.

D. What an example! We, like Isaiah, cannot come into God's holy presence and remain the same.

Conclusion

Whether it's the "holy, holy, holy" of Isa. 6:3 in the Old Testament or of Rev. 4:8 in the New Testament, the idea is the same. God is holy at the very core of His being.

A Picture of God's Holiness

Isaiah 6:3

Introduction

How does the Bible picture God's holiness? As we look at the biblical terms used in reference to God's holiness we discover three main ideas.

I. God Is High and Lifted Up

A. The Bible often describes God as sitting on a majestic throne. In the Old Testament great power and authority were attributed to a king's throne (see 1 Kings 7:7; 2 Chron. 9:17-19).

    1. God has just such a throne in heaven.

    2. From this throne our holy God watches over all creation.

B. The psalmist describes it well in 47:8 and 89:14.

    1. These twin foundations of God's throne remind us that He always does what is right and judges those who do wrong.

    2. The concepts of doing right and judgment for wrongdoing fold into a biblical concept of God's holiness.

II. God Shines as a Bright Light

A. "There the angel of the LORD appeared to him in flames of fire from within a bush" (Exod. 3:2).

    1. He imaged himself to Moses as a bright fire in the burning bush.

    2. At the giving of the Ten Commandments God descended on Mount Sinai as a bright fire (see 19:18).

    3. When Moses asked God if he could see His glory, God indicated that His glory was too bright for human eyes, so God compromised and allowed him to see His back as He passed by (see 33:23).

4. Moses' own encounter with God's glory, though brief, made his own face shine with a bright glow. He had to wear a veil over his face when he talked to the Israelites (see 34:29-35).

B. Following their departure from Egypt, God lived with His children in the Tabernacle and filled it with His glory. Moses and the people could not enter the holy place because it was so filled with the presence of the Lord (see 40:34-35).

III. God Is Pure

A. "Everyone who has this hope in him purifies himself, just as he is pure" (1 John 3:3).

B. He does not defile himself with sin or anything that would dilute His character (see Hab. 1:13).

C. God calls us to the same purity (see Ps. 73:1; Matt. 5:8).

Conclusion

These three concepts give us a clearer picture of God's holiness: God is high and lifted up, God shines as a bright light, and God is pure.

SET APART FOR GOD

Leviticus 20:26

Introduction

A holy God reserves things for himself. He sets things apart for His use or enjoyment. They remain separate from the secular or profane. They are not the run-of-the-mill discount-store closeout items. They are special because they belong to God.

I. Things Set Apart

A. The high priest's garments (see Exod. 28:2)

B. The Tabernacle and all the objects in it (see 40:9)

C. The tithe (see Lev. 27:32)

D. The Sabbath (see Exod. 35:2-3; Isa. 58:13)

E. Jerusalem (see Isa. 48:2)

F. The Temple (see Matt. 24:15)

G. Scripture (see Rom. 1:2)

II. The Priestly Concept of Holiness

The concept of something being holy because it is set apart for God is often referred to as the priestly concept of holiness.

1. This is because priests themselves personified the Tabernacle or Temple, and all of the objects in the Tabernacle and Temple were associated with the worship of God.

2. Everything set apart for God received reverence.

III. The Priestly Concept of Holiness Applied to God's Creation

A. The Tabernacle and Temple, along with all of the objects associated with the worship of God, belonged to Him and thus were set apart for His holy purposes.

B. We see in this God's desire to share His holiness with His creation.
   1. Separated from the world and sin (see Rom. 8:5-8)
   2. Separated to God (see Lev. 20:26; Ps. 4:3)
   3. Separated for service (see Titus 2:14)

Conclusion

We, too, can belong to Him and can be set apart for Him. We, too, can become holy. Being set apart for God is a biblical concept that originates in God's holiness.

A Fatal Infection

Romans 5:12

Introduction

Adam and Eve were given the option of self-sovereignty or surrender of self-preference to the Creator's will. They chose self-sovereignty. With that choice came the knowledge of good and evil and an awareness of disobeying God. This choice created a change in the hearts of the first parents and in the hearts of all of their future children. Now, instead of initially preferring God's will and plan, they prefer their own.

I. Who Is Infected? (Rom. 5:12)

A. Every one of us gets this infection just by being born into the world.
  1. It is the universal problem of sin.
  2. It is a very part of our nature from the garden days.
B. Every time we defy God's will and break God's heart, we affirm our preference for self-sovereignty.

II. Bad News (Gen. 3:22)

We are infected.
  1. What can we do to help ourselves?
  2. We can exercise large quantities of willpower, or we can turn over a tree full of new leaves, but that is about all.

III. Good News (Luke 1:69, 74-75)

Here is the good news—the message of holiness.
  1. Not only can God forgive us of our past sins, but He can also change us from within and reorient our nature so we can return to His will and plan for our lives.
  2. He heals us of "the infection."

Conclusion

The bad news is, "We're infected." The good news is, "God can heal us." He restores us to the way He originally intended us to be in the garden. Now we are no longer deprived of His presence. Now we are forgiven of self-preference. Now we can be what God wants us to be. We can't do this ourselves but by the strength and power of His Holy Spirit living within us.

Holiness—a Miracle of Grace

Luke 1:69, 74-75

Introduction

How does God work a miracle of grace on "the infection" with which sin grips me? That is somewhat of a spiritual mystery. God first requires the expectation of our faith. Just as I trusted Christ to forgive my past sins, so I trust Him to accept when I offer myself more fully to Him. This miracle starts with an offer we make in seeking God's full will for our lives.

I. Consecration (Rom. 12:1)

Our offer is called consecration.

1. Consecration is when we present ourselves to God in a new and sacrificial way.
2. Consecration involves our act of making ourselves available to God as a component of our worship of Him.

II. Sanctification (1 Thess. 5:23-24)

A. "Sanctification" and related words, such as "sanctify," "holy," and "holiness" occur in the Bible more than 1,100 times.
B. Sanctification refers to a total, lifelong process of becoming holy.
   1. It is all God does in us to restore our hearts to the way He created us to be.
   2. The point at which God sanctifies us wholly refers to a particular point in time when we consecrate ourselves fully to God and give up the stronghold of self-preference.
      a. My spiritual self-seeking, self-willed, self-sufficient ways have to go.

        b. Selfishness is replaced by a new availability to all God wants for me.

III. Holiness (Luke 1:75)

    A. Holiness is the condition of our soul and characterization of our lifestyle that results from God's work in sanctification. Whatever He asks me to do, I am willing to do.

    B. Holiness comes from an old English word also translated "whole," "health," or "hallow."

    C. Holiness is being whole, in good health, or holy.

Conclusion

The miracle of a holy life begins with consecration. Consecration is our part. Sanctification is God's part. Holiness is the miracle that cures "the infection."

The Symbol and Its Reality

Hebrews 10:1-4

Introduction

The Old Testament sacrifice was designed to bring people to God and make them right in His sight. The animals died, the blood spilled, and the meat was offered to the flames. Yet the people went home year after year without feeling any different inside, not knowing if their sins were actually forgiven. The ritual did not seem to change anything deep inside their souls.

I. The Symbol (v. 4)

The sacrificial system did well at defining the sin problem.

1. It made people feel guilty when they measured their lives against the law.
2. It pointed to their deep spiritual need and hunger.
3. It couldn't get down deep enough to solve the problem, actually forgive the sins, and bring inner freedom.
4. It only pointed worshipers in the right direction, set them on a journey, then left them stranded along the roadside.

II. The Reality (v. 9)

A. When Christ came, He changed all of that.
   1. His sacrifice of himself became the best sacrifice of all, the most complete in every way.
   2. The perfect Son of God completed the entire Old Testament sacrificial system with His own sacrifice.
   3. He replaced the symbol with the reality.

B. Something wonderful happens in us as a result of this perfect sacrifice (see v. 10).

III. The Secret of Holiness (see v. 14)

A. Our holiness has its root in Jesus Christ's obedience to the Father's salvation plan. According to that plan Jesus offered himself as a sacrifice for the world's sins—He obeyed the Father.

B. We identify with Christ and sacrifice ourselves to God just as He did.

   1. God accepts our efforts, not as efforts on our own strength, but as faith steps of following our perfect Example, Jesus, and letting Him direct us.

   2. Jesus Christ, the Holy One, lives in and through us and, in doing so, makes us holy—His life in us.

Conclusion

Here we find the message of full salvation from sin. Here we see God's plan to bring us back to himself. We don't have to wait for the death angel's knock to receive this blessed hope. Through Christ's sacrifice on the Cross we can find our sins forgiven, be identified with the perfect sacrifice, and receive holiness of heart. Here is the secret to full salvation from sin—both forgiveness of acts of sinning (sin problem No. 1) and the inclination to sin in the first place (sin problem No. 2). It is all made possible by Christ's sacrifice.

The Holy Sprit Promised

Acts 1:4-5

Introduction

Jesus stood on the Mount of Olives telling His disciples good-bye. Their hearts sagged with sorrow. They could hardly find proper words to close their time together. Then He filled their ears and hearts with a message of promise and hope.

I. The Promise Is Given

He promised a new source of power for their Christian lives (see 1:8).

   1. They obeyed.
   2. They prayed.
   3. They waited.
   4. They were united.

II. The Promise Fulfilled

The sights and sounds of Pentecost signaled God's presence and power (see 2:1-4).

   1. A great wind blew through their prayer meeting, symbolizing power.
   2. Flames of fire descended upon each prayer-meeting participant, symbolizing purity of heart.
   3. The disciples began proclaiming the gospel message in languages they had never learned.

III. The Coming of the Holy Spirit to the Believer's Heart

The Scriptures indicate several things about the coming of the Holy Spirit into a person's life.

   1. It begins with waiting in prayerful anticipation.

2. It comes by having faith that God wants to do something for the individual.
3. It brings purity of heart.
4. It brings power for Christian service and witness.

Conclusion

Though the disciples were filled with sorrow and disappointment as Jesus left them to return to the Father, they were now filled with joy and power because of the coming of the Comforter. So when the Holy Spirit comes to the heart of the believer, he or she is filled with joy and power to go into the world to live and witness for Christ.

An Old Promise

Isaiah 6:1-8

Introduction

During the period of the Old Testament sacrificial system, God gave His prophets glorious promises and images of what would happen someday when His Holy Spirit would arrive.

I. Isaiah's Vision (see Isa. 6:1-8; 44:3)

II. Jeremiah's Vision (see Jer. 31:31-33)

III. Ezekiel's Vision (see Ezek. 36:23-27)

IV. Joel's Vision (see Joel 2:28-29)

Conclusion

We see from these visions of God's prophets that God had been planning this special gift of the Holy Spirit for a long, long time. What Jesus promised His disciples on the Mount of Olives just before His ascension simply restated a promise that God had been making to His servants across the years.

Divine Transformation

Romans 5:12—6:19

Introduction

Jesus undid the damage of the garden Fall and opened a new way for us to relate to God. That new way is made possible by the coming of the Holy Spirit at Pentecost. Consider the transformation that takes place.

I. The Problem of the Sin Nature (see 5:12-14)

A. Paul begins this passage by addressing our problem with the sin nature.

B. Adam and Eve's sinful choice threw all humanity out of balance with God and themselves.

II. The Sin Nature Broken (see vv. 19-21)

A. Christ came as a second Adam, exposed himself to the same temptations to sin, and obeyed God. He did what Adam and Eve did not do, then went to the Cross to purchase our salvation, thus undoing Adam and Eve's damage.

B. After sin's power over us is broken, we are freed to live a new kind of life by identifying with Christ in His crucifixion, and our old life of sin dies.

III. Transformed to Christlikeness (see 6:1-10)

Since Christ by His death on the Cross undid the garden damage, then spiritually speaking we're back to square one with God's original plan.

1. We can now be like Christ (see v. 11).
   a. That means we are to live as if God's new life really is at work in us (see v. 12).
   b. Since we chose to sin, we can now choose not to sin.

2. We replace that old lifestyle with full devotion to God (see v. 13). This results in lives characterized by right living.

Conclusion

Where does this new life with God lead? Paul gives the answer in 6:19—it is "righteousness leading to holiness." It is a life of Christlikeness.

The Way to Holiness

Romans 6

Introduction

Maturity and growth are natural to the life of holiness—and especially after the coming of the Holy Spirit in His fullness. Let us note some challenges from Rom. 6 for nurturing the life of holiness.

I. "Count Yourselves Dead to Sin" (v. 11)

A. That means we are to live as if God's new life really is at work in us.

B. It means believing in the power of God to do as He promised and really change us.

II. "Do Not Let Sin Reign" (v. 12)

A. Christ has broken the power of that reign through His death on the Cross; we identify with His death on the Cross.

B. God creates the possibility; we respond by living the reality.

C. Since we chose to sin, we can now choose not to sin.

III. "Do Not Offer the Parts of Your Body to Sin" (v. 13)

A. We leave the old sinful lifestyle behind; we move away leaving no forwarding address.

B. We replace the old lifestyle with full devotion to God.

C. This change results in lives characterized by right living.

IV. "Righteousness Leading to Holiness" (vv. 19, 22)

A. That is where Paul's argument has been leading all along.

B. "The benefit you reap leads to holiness, and the result is eternal life" (v. 22).

Conclusion

All along the way we grow in our relationship with God. That growth takes place on the road of holiness.

Characteristics of the Sin Nature

Introduction

There are characteristics of the sin nature that will be a destructive force to the believer who seeks to become Christlike. The core of self-centeredness must be surrendered to the cleansing of the Holy Spirit. Consider these characteristics:

I. Self-Centered

Acting as if the earth and all other planets in this universe revolve around you

II. Self-Assertive

Moving to the front of the line because you deserve to be first; having to win every table game

III. Self-Deprecation

Calling undue attention to yourself by putting yourself down to get others to praise you

IV. Conceited

Acting as if you are God's gift to humanity

V. Self-Indulgent

Looking primarily after your own wants and needs

VI. Self-Pleasing

Making sure your family or group eats where you want to eat and watches the television program you want to watch—every time

VII. Self-Seeking

Being so in love with yourself that your primary responsibility in life is to assure your own happiness

VIII. Self-Pity

Feeling sorry for yourself because you are so deprived

IX. Defensive

Always making excuses to justify your behavior

X. Self-Sufficiency

Living as if you need no one else's help, not even God's

XI. Self-Consciousness

Being so concerned about how you look or the impression you make on others that you accomplish little else; always worrying about what other people think

XII. Self-Preoccupied

Being so focused on your own interests and needs that you are not aware of the world around you

XIII. Self-Introspective

Going around all day with your finger on your psychological, emotional, or spiritual pulse and monitoring every wavelength that passes through your brain

XIV. Self-Righteous

Getting blessed at the incredible blessing and contribution you are to God's work and being proud of your good example

XV. Self-Glorying

Calling attention to your ministry and spiritual accomplishments and amazing even yourself at just how good you are

XVI. Self-Proclaiming

Announcing to everyone that you are God's answer to folks' prayers and declaring your ways to be God's wishes in a particular situation

XVII. Self-Made

Being proud of the fact that no one gave you money or support in helping you get to where you are today

Conclusion

What is the result of this pattern of thinking and living? It damages and destroys relationships with family and friends. It short-circuits concern for others. It ultimately results in loneliness and unfulfillment. It leaves a wake of evil and corruption.

The Holy Spirit

John 14:16

Introduction

Jesus taught us most of what we know about the Holy Spirit in John 14—17. These chapters contain the five Paraclete sayings of Jesus about the coming of the Holy Spirit. *Paraklētos* is the Greek word usually translated "comforter," "counselor," "advocate," or "helper." The literal meaning is, "the one called alongside." In looking at all of the English words translated from the Greek word *paraklētos,* we gain new insight into the Holy Spirit's ministry.

I. Another Counselor (See 14:15-18)

The gift of the Father, the Spirit of Truth, lives with and within so that we are not abandoned as orphans.

II. The Teacher (See v. 26)

The Father sent the Teacher to remind us of all the things we were taught.

III. The Witness (See 15:26)

The Father sent the Spirit of Truth to testify of Jesus.

IV. Convicting the World (See 16:8-11)

The Father sent the Spirit of Truth to convict the world of guilt.

1. Sin
2. Righteousness
3. Judgment

V. The Guide (See v. 13)

The Spirit speaks only what He hears.

Conclusion

Jesus brought glory to His Father during His earthly ministry. John 16:14 says, "He will bring glory to me by taking from what is mine and making it known to you." We see the Spirit bringing glory to the Son. The Son takes spiritual insight on living from His Father; the Spirit takes this insight and passes it on to us. What an incredible privilege we enjoy through the ministry of the Holy Spirit.

When Can One Be Sanctified?

1 Thessalonians 5:23-24

Introduction

When can one honestly expect to be sanctified? Airlines provide the ETA (estimated time of arrival) for their flights. We cannot predict the ETA for sanctification as an airline can. It's far too complex. Spiritual development is different for different individuals. People have different backgrounds, upbringings, education, and experiences. We also have different personalities. And people interpret Scripture passages about sanctification differently. Let us consider some of the different views.

I. Sanctification Happens After a Person Dies

This interpretation views heaven as a perfect place. In order to keep us from polluting it the moment we step foot through the doorway, this view holds that God must do something to make us holy or fit for our new perfect environment. It stands to reason that God must accomplish this holy work in us after we die. This view makes sense, but it is not biblical. There are hundreds of references to sanctification that speak of a present reality.

II. Sanctification Happens Just Before a Person Dies

This interpretation sees us growing incrementally in God's sanctifying grace throughout life. Sometime just before our earthly departure, God graduates us from the growth process and grants us sanctification. This prepares us to enter heaven's perfection. Because it happens at the time of death, we call it "dying grace." Such a view sounds logical, but it has no biblical basis. It has biblical and logical problems. All explanations of dying grace make it sound like something automatic rather than a gift received from God by faith, which is the biblical position.

III. Sanctification Happens Instantaneously at the Time God Forgives Us of Our Sins and Gives Us New Birth

This interpretation joins the new birth and sanctification as twin gifts of God granted simultaneously like a coin with two sides. When we ask God for forgiveness of sins and accept Christ as Savior, we receive regeneration and sanctification. This view does not see believers growing in holiness throughout life but simply living within the gift granted at the beginning of the Christian life.

The problem with this view is not only God's inability to grant us multiple levels of grace at one time but also our inability to comprehend multiple levels of understanding at the same time. God deals with us at every stage of our spiritual journey according to the level of our comprehension. God works with us according to our developmental ability.

IV. Sanctification Begins When God Forgives Us of Our Sins and Gives Us New Birth, and It Grows Incrementally Throughout the Rest of Our Lives on Earth

This interpretation sees sanctification as progressive over the long haul of living. As the believer reads the Bible, prays, attends church services, and turns to other channels of God's grace, he or she becomes more aware of the sinful nature still residing deep within the heart. Being grieved by this sinful nature, the believer enters a conflict between flesh and spirit. The result is a constant uphill struggle. It leaves us with a lifelong struggle against the sinful nature. Worst of all, it calls for us to grow out of selfishness or self-centeredness. Only God's cleansing work can adequately deal with the culprit.

V. Sanctification Begins in the New Birth, Grows with the Spiritual Development to the Time of a Second Moment When the Spirit Takes Complete Control, Then Develops Incrementally in Maturity Throughout a Believer's Life

God's transforming work begins in us the moment He forgives us of our past sins and gives us new birth. We call this *initial sanctification.* Spiritual and personal growth occur each time we make a godly decision or resist a temptation. We call this *progressive sanctification.*

At some point we rendezvous with a moment when we must come to terms more decisively than ever before with Christ's claims of Lordship on us. In loving response we offer ourselves a living sacrifice for God and His service (Rom. 12:1-2). God accepts our consecration and sanctifies every part of our being (1 Thess. 5:23-24). We call this moment *entire sanctification.*

Conclusion

This last interpretation incorporates the main biblical references to sanctification and holiness. This is the Wesleyan interpretation of sanctification.

WHAT THE BIBLE SAYS ABOUT SANCTIFICATION

Introduction

There are many biblical directives concerning our sanctification. Let us notice some of the central features the Scriptures give.

I. A Baptism

A baptism as an event in time (see Matt. 3:11)

II. A Seal

The Holy Spirit impressing His signet ring on the warm wax of our soul in a moment (see Eph. 1:13; 2 Cor. 1:22)

III. A Down Payment

A down payment placed on a piece of property, promising full payment to come (2 Cor. 1:22)

IV. A Circumcision of the Heart

A circumcision of the heart that happens in a moment (see Rom. 2:29; Col. 2:9-15)

V. A Crucifixion of the Old Sinful Nature

A crucifixion of the old sinful nature as a decisive event in time (see Rom. 6:6; Gal. 2:20)

VI. A Cleansing Act

As Christ cleansed the church "by the washing with water through the word" (Eph. 5:25-27)

VII. A Clothing with Spiritual Power

An event of clothing "with power from on high" (Luke 24:49)

VIII. An Invitation

An invitation to live under the full direction of the Helper (see John 14—17)

IX. A Death to Sin

Dead to self and sin, alive to full life in God (see Rom. 6:11)

X. A Consecration of Self

An act of offering "your bodies as living sacrifices" (Rom. 12:1-2)

XI. A Temple of the Holy Spirit

When God's spirit lives in you, you become God's temple (see 1 Cor. 3:16-17; 6:19-20).

XII. A Purification

A purification from all uncleanness and "perfecting holiness out of reverence for God" (2 Cor. 7:1)

XIII. Taking Off Dirty Clothes and Putting on Clean Ones

"Put off [the] old self," and "put on the new self" (see Eph. 4:22-24).

XIV. A Renewable Spirit Filling

Being filled with the Holy Spirit (see Eph. 5:18)

XV. A Work of Completion

Being sanctified "through and through" (1 Thess. 5:23-24)

XVI. The Acceptance of a Call

"But just as he who has called you is holy, so be holy in all you do; for it is written: 'Be holy, because I am holy'" (1 Pet. 1:15-16).

Conclusion

Sanctification brings about a radical change in the life of the believer. It prepares the believer to travel the way of holiness. The result will be a life of growth as the Christian grows with the Holy Spirit as guide.

Goals in the Life of Holiness, Part One

Introduction

God moves us in the direction of maturity throughout our lives and works in various ways in the following areas of life. To each of these areas the Holy Spirit offers direction and helps us in necessary improvements.

I. **Loving God and Others with Our Entire Being**

II. **Using Free Will to Choose God's Ways and Avoid Evil Choices and Attitudes**

III. **Relating Well to Others, Tolerant of Social and Personal Differences**

IV. **Preferring the Needs of Others Over Our Own Needs**

V. **Showing Compassion to Needy People**

Conclusion

As we follow the Holy Spirit's guidance, we will reach new goals. Some of these may be more easily attainable than others. But the believer experiences the help of the Holy Spirit in attaining new levels of maturity.

GOALS IN THE LIFE OF HOLINESS, PART TWO

Introduction

As we continue our journey to reach new goals in the life of holiness, we will see that holiness reaches every area of the believer's life. Some of these goals will require time and diligence to attain.

 I. **Emotional Stability**

 II. **Coping Skills to Adjust to the Difficulties and Changing Circumstances of Life**

 III. **Accepting Our Sexuality and Practicing Proper Expression Within Biblical Guidelines**

 IV. **Proper Management of Money and Material Possessions**

 V. **Proper Understanding of Risks, Danger, and Death**

 VI. **Effective Management of Time**

 VII. **Proper Balance Between Work and Play, Responsibility and Recreation**

VIII. **Proper Understanding of Our Skills and Abilities**

Conclusion

The goals set before the sanctified believer are challenging and require obedience and openness to the Holy Spirit.

GOALS IN THE LIFE OF HOLINESS, PART THREE

Introduction

A drive through the mountains often reveals new wonders at the next turn or the next level. A person may climb to new heights only to find at the next turn there is another pass to reach. So it is with the life of holiness. There are always new heights to gain as we reach the goals set before us. Consider these goals:

I. **Ability to Live with Ambiguity and Unanswered Questions in Life**

II. **Growing Discernment of and Sensitivity to Evil and the Subtle Ways It Tempts Believers**

III. **Ability to Discern Between Essentials and Nonessentials**

IV. **Sacrificing the Good for the Best**

V. **Establishing Priorities from Wishful Desires**

VI. **Training Our Conscience and Remaining Sensitive to It**

Conclusion

As we strive to reach the goals set before us, we mature in the life of holiness. Christlikeness is our overarching aim.

Goals in the Life of Holiness, Part Four

Introduction

Entire sanctification begins in a moment of time, but the process of applying it to all aspects of life takes a lifetime. God helps us to change the things we need to change. In doing this, He helps us reach new goals in the life of holiness.

I. **Being Aware of Our Appetites, Passions, and Drives in Order to Control Them Properly**

II. **Being Aware of Our Weaknesses, Prejudices, and Negative Tendencies in Order to Develop or Correct Them**

III. **Understanding Our Normal Mood Swings, Learning to Control the Highs and Lows of the Cycle So As Not to Create Stress on Family and Friends**

IV. **Willfully Accepting Persecution for the Cause of Christ**

V. **Properly Understanding Our Place in the World**

VI. **Properly Understanding the Purpose of Life and Being Governed by a Personal Life Philosophy**

Conclusion

Reaching goals in the life of holiness takes a lifetime. God helps us in ways we call the means of grace. Some of the means of grace are prayer, meditation, attending faithfully the worship services, fellowship, and selfless service. With the apostle Paul, let us reach for the goal that is before us. Mother Teresa said, "My progress in holiness depends on God and myself: on God's grace and my will."*

---

*Mother Teresa, *Total Surrender,* ed. Brother Angelo Devananda (Ann Arbor, Mich.: Servant Publications, 1985), 31.

The Goal of Holiness—Christlikeness, Part One

Introduction

The goal of holiness is Christlikeness. Paul states it clearly in 2 Cor. 3:18. This series of sermons will help us see a picture of what God's Son is like and the many aspects of Christlikeness we can emulate.

I. Jesus Loved the Father First and Foremost, Then He Loved Us as an Outgrowth of Their Love for Each Other (See Matt. 22:37-40)

II. Jesus Had a *Winsome Personality*

   A. Crowds pressed Him by the thousands (see John 6:1-2).

   1. Something about His life and conversation attracted them like metal shavings to a magnet.

   2. They wanted to hear what He had to say and see Him in action.

   B. He helped people feel at ease in His presence. Many people, like Nicodemus, opened up and shared their hearts with Him (see John 3:1-21).

III. Jesus Lived a Life of Humility

   A. Jesus did not put himself down, but He gave himself away to meet others' needs. He even talked about being lowly in spirit as a virtue for us to emulate (see Matt. 11:29).

   B. Once His disciples argued among themselves about which of them was greater. Jesus illustrated the error of their thinking by placing a child among them and stressing the virtue of childlikeness (see Matt. 18:1-5).

   C. When James and John sought to rule with Him in His coming kingdom, Jesus pointed out that those who want to rule over all must become humble servants of all (see Mark 10:43-45).

   D. Then, at the Last Supper, He washed His disciples' feet as a humble example for us all (see John 13:2-17).

IV. Jesus Lived a Balanced Life

Jesus worked, rested, spent time with others, took time to be alone, socialized with saints and sinners, and enjoyed the give-and-take of daily life.

1. He was neither a workaholic nor a man of leisure.
2. He stayed busy, but He knew when to stop and rest.

V. Jesus Had a Sense of Humor

Jesus wasn't always seriously preaching and teaching.

1. He mixed a great deal of humor with His personal conversation and formal messages.
2. He spoke of seeing a splinter while tripping over a large board (see Matt. 7:3).
3. He joked about tediously straining a gnat out of a drink then swallowing a camel (see 23:24).
4. Try to picture those images without laughing.

Conclusion

God wants to make us like His Son, Jesus Christ. Colossians 1:27 says, "God has chosen to make known among the Gentiles the glorious riches of this mystery, which is Christ in you, the hope of glory." Paul expressed his desire for the Galatians that Christ be "formed" in them (Gal. 4:19).

The Goal of Holiness—Christlikeness, Part Two

Introduction

We must constantly seek to become more like Christ. We live as God wants us to live and seek to become more like His Son because we love Him. We want to honor Him in all we do. Peter reminds us that as we do this, we participate in Christ's divine nature (2 Pet. 1:4).

I. Jesus Had a Heart of Compassion and Gave His Hands to Compassionate Ministry

As He walked and talked with the crowds of people who followed Him, Jesus' heart reached out to their hurts and needs.

1. Anyone who came to Jesus found a listening ear and an outstretched hand.
2. He sympathized with people and did what He could to help them (see Matt. 8:14-17).

II. Jesus Lived a Life of Fairness

He defended His disciples when others wrongly accused them but also scolded them when they were wrong (see Mark 2:23-28). For example, He criticized Peter when Peter rebuked Jesus for predicting His death but praised Peter for recognizing Him as "the Christ, the Son of the living God" (Matt. 16:13-23).

III. Jesus Was Courteous

He spoke with dignity and respect to society's outcasts and those with sinful pasts.

1. People's stations in life did not impress Jesus.
2. He treated the rich, poor, educated, uneducated, important, and disenfranchised all the same.
3. As a Jewish male Jesus conversed with a Samaritan female in public—a forbidden social practice. At the end of the religious discussion, Jesus led her to a relationship with God.

4. Jesus knew everyone needed a relationship with His Father (see John 4:4-26).

IV. Jesus Was Thoughtful

In the confusion of Jesus' arrest in the Garden of Gethsemane, Peter lashed out with his sword and cut off Malchus's ear. Jesus miraculously healed Malchus (see Luke 22:50-51).

V. Jesus Paid Compliments and Showed Appreciation

Jesus paid a high compliment to a sinful woman and created a social scene at the home of a Pharisee when the woman honored Jesus by anointing His feet with alabaster perfume and wiping them with her hair (see Luke 7:36-50).

Conclusion

O to be like Thee! blessed Redeemer—
This is my constant longing and prayer.
Gladly I'll forfeit all of earth's treasures,
Jesus, Thy perfect likeness to wear.

—Thomas O. Chisholm

THE GOAL OF HOLINESS—CHRISTLIKENESS, PART THREE

Introduction

Christlikeness is the goal for the Spirit-filled believer. Paul in 2 Cor. 3:18 expresses it this way: "And we, who with unveiled faces all reflect the Lord's glory, are being transformed into his likeness with ever-increasing glory, which comes from the Lord, who is the Spirit." Let us look again at His life that is our pattern.

I. Jesus Did Not Try to Create Conflict with His Enemies, but When It Arose, He Did Not Run from It

A. The Pharisees, at one point, prepared to do battle with Jesus, so He moved His ministry from Judea back through Samaria to Galilee (see John 4:1-3). However, when the chief priests and teachers of the law tried to trip Him with a trick question, He stood up to them and refused to answer their question (see Luke 20:1-8).

B. Another time, Jesus publicly broke a Sabbath rule to make a point with a Pharisee (see 14:1-5).

II. Jesus Did Not Contemplate His Plight in Life and Feel Sorry for Himself

A. He lived with the shame and slander surrounding society's notion of His illegitimate birth.

B. He acknowledged personal rejection by His hometown community.

C. He lived with constant opposition from His enemies.

D. His brothers and sisters did not honor Him during His ministry.

E. His own disciples did not understand Him most of the time, yet He did not assume a victim mentality, blame others, or feel sorry for himself (see Luke 23:28-31).

III. Jesus Was Not Vindictive and Did Not Retaliate When Others Treated Him Wrongly

He urged us to turn the other cheek to wrongdoers, give to

those who rob us, and go the second mile with those who impose on our kindness (see Matt. 5:38-48).

IV. Jesus Did Not Need to Make a Name for Himself

He preached, taught, and healed in the midst of all who came to Him, but He never attempted to create fame or fortune for himself as an outgrowth of His successful ministry (see Matt. 12:11-16). In fact, He actually sought to keep His popularity from growing (see v. 16).

V. Jesus Expressed Strong Emotion and Imagination When the Occasion Called for It

Jesus did not get angry over selfish concerns or become self-defensive over personal attacks, but He did react strongly at times.

1. For example, He created quite a scene in the Temple area over the money changers and dove sellers (see Matt. 21:12-13).
2. He also became upset when His disciples tried to keep children away from His ministry (see Mark 10:13-16).

Conclusion

Earthly pleasures vainly call me;
I would be like Jesus;
Nothing worldly shall enthrall me;
I would be like Jesus.

Be like Jesus, this my song,
In the home and in the throng;
Be like Jesus, all day long!
I would be like Jesus.

—James Rowe

The Goal of Holiness—Christlikeness, Part Four

Introduction

God's goal for the believer is holiness. But He needed an example to set before us. He needed a picture of the goal—a picture we could keep before us. He did just that. He framed us a picture of His Son and said, "Become like Him." That's what Paul meant when he said, "For those God foreknew he also predestined to be conformed to the likeness of his Son, that he might be the firstborn among many brothers" (Rom. 8:29).

I. Jesus Showed Great Courage Throughout His Life

A. He faced Satan's frontal attacks during 40 days of temptation.

B. He courageously began His public ministry in the shadow of His popular cousin John's ministry.

C. He publicly opposed the traditional laws that were inhumane and ungodly.

D. He countered the religious leaders in their errors.

E. He called sin by its real name and pointed to it in others' lives.

F. He refused to lower himself to the demands of the people to crown Him as their king.

G. He courageously accepted the Father's plan for His life even though it meant going to the Cross.

II. Jesus Had a Clear Mission and Purpose for His Life

A. This mission and purpose was clearly in place by the time He first visited the Temple at the age of 12 (see Luke 2:49).

B. He carried this vision with Him throughout His earthly ministry (see 4:18-19).

C. He worked daily with a sense of urgency.

D. He envisioned the harvest of souls at hand and did all He could to bring that harvest to His Father (see John 4:34-38).

III. Jesus Lived with Eternity's Values in View

Jesus kept His feet firmly planted on the ground but never lost sight of heaven's view.

   1. Every event from the beginning of His ministry to the Cross gave Him opportunity to show how to respond in light of eternity's values.
   2. Every word He said and every miracle He performed somehow related to God's eternal purposes.

IV. Jesus Realized and Accepted His Human Limitations

   A. When His body grew weary, He stopped and rested.
   B. When He reached a point of exhaustion, He withdrew from society and spent time alone.
   C. When His burden grew heavy in the Garden of Gethsemane, He sought His disciples' help in carrying the load.

V. Jesus Always Sought to Do His Father's Will

   A. He demonstrated this perspective at age 12 (see Luke 2:49).
   B. At Gethsemane He obviously carried through with what His Father wanted (see Matt. 26:39, 42).
   C. More than anything, He wanted to see His Father's will accomplished (see John 4:34; 6:38).

Conclusion

We must also seek continually to do the Father's will. The songwriter wrote,

> That in heaven He may meet me,
> I would be like Jesus;
> That His words, "Well done," may greet me,
> I would be like Jesus.
>
> —James Rowe

Our goal is Christlikeness.

The Goal of Holiness—Christlikeness, Part Five

Introduction

Trying to describe the picture of God's Son is like trying to capture the majesty of the Grand Canyon with a five-dollar disposable camera. That doesn't mean we shouldn't make an attempt at it. Look again at the picture before us.

I. Jesus Lived in Constant Communion with His Father

Prayer remained a constant source of strength for Jesus.

1. He started His ministry in prayer (see Luke 6:12).
2. He spent extended seasons of prayer after particularly taxing events (see Mark 6:46).
3. He called attention to the importance of prayer before performing miracles (John 11:41-42).

II. Jesus Depended on the Holy Spirit for Constant Spiritual Strength and Encouragement

A. The Spirit filled Jesus to adequately prepare Him for His battle with Satan's temptations (see Luke 4:1-2).

B. Jesus accomplished everything through the power of God's Spirit working through Him.

C. He prayed that His disciples and followers would have the same Spirit working in them (see John 17:1-26).

III. Jesus Lived a Life of Service

A. He always found ways to give himself in service to those who needed Him.

B. He set the example for His followers.

C. He left an admonition to selfless service in the parable of the sheep and the goats (see Matt. 25:32-33). "I tell you the truth, whatever you did for one of the least of these brothers of mine, you did for me" (v. 40).

D. After washing His disciples' feet, Jesus said, "I have set you an example that you should do as I have done for you" (John 13:15).

IV. Jesus Submitted Himself to Suffering on Our Behalf

A. Jesus' sufferings are clearly documented throughout the New Testament Gospels.

B. Paul reminds us of our part in sharing in His suffering (see 2 Cor. 1:5; Phil 3:10).

C. Peter also realized the need for us to follow Christ's example (see 1 Pet. 2:21).

V. Jesus Submitted Himself to Death on the Cross to Accomplish Our Salvation

A. Christ's death on the Cross opened the way for us to live in vital relationship with the Father.

B. Christ's crucifixion symbolizes the importance of our own daily crucifixion to self-will (see Gal 2:20).

C. It further reminds us that if we live and witness for Christ, we will pay the price along with Him.

D. We must always remember Jesus' words to His disciples in Matt. 16:24, "If anyone would come after me, he must deny himself and take up his cross and follow me."

Conclusion

Our challenge is found in Heb. 12:2. We must "fix our eyes" on Jesus and depend on His Holy Spirit to work His transforming miracle through us as we remain open to His work in our lives. Each day we seek, as John says, to "walk as Jesus did" (1 John 2:6).

The Marks of Holiness, Part One

Introduction

God does many wonderful things in our spiritual walk with Him as we bring His plan to reality in our lives. God works with us as individuals, so no two believers' experiences with God will be identical. God's timetable is seeker-sensitive to an individual's need and openness to Him. Never get discouraged because growth is not as quick as you would like.

I. Holiness Makes Us More Sensitive to the Holy Spirit's Leading in Our Lives

A. We become more aware of God's direction, more in tune with the gentle Voice guiding our choices.

  1. This fulfills the images that God gave His prophets about how things would be when the Holy Spirit filled followers.

     a. Isa. 44:3

     b. Jer. 31:31-33

     c. Ezek. 36:23, 25-27

     d. Joel 2:28-29

  2. Not only do these passages speak of heart cleansing from the spiritual infection that hinders our progress, but also they speak of an internal awareness of God's will and plan for us.

B. God only asks that we seek Him and welcome His presence in our lives more than anything. With that open invitation, He willingly gives us new insight for daily living.

II. Holiness Gives Us a New and Deeper Love for God and Others

A. Love becomes an affection and a principle of life for us.

B. We seek to love God more than anything. When we see something else taking that supreme place in our lives, we quickly lower its position and restore God to first place.

C. We begin to see people as God sees them.

1. We genuinely care about their needs and find ways to meet those needs.
2. The driving force of this love is not a great deal of extra effort on our part but the love of God flowing through us.
   a. The reason we call it "perfect love" is not that it responds perfectly in every situation but because it comes from God and reaches to His hurting world.
   b. It contains no mixture of selfish ambition.
D. We strive to love others the way the Father loves His Son and the way the Son loves us.
   1. We become channels through whom His love flows.
   2. We love others with a love God gives us, as described in 1 Cor. 13.

Conclusion

God works with each believer on an individual basis. His timetable and way of working with each of us will be somewhat different. Doing God's will brings great fulfillment, satisfaction, and spiritual fruit. That fruit of God's work is the mark of holiness.

THE MARKS OF HOLINESS, PART TWO

Introduction

Holiness helps us realize the Holy Spirit's work in our lives to make us more loving, humble, and spiritually sensitive. He wants us to conform to the image of His Son, Jesus Christ. Let's continue to look at marks of holiness in the life of the believer.

I. Holiness Gives Us a New Level of Humility and Awareness of the Grace of God at Work in Us

Perhaps the chief enemy to humility is self-centeredness.

1. Self keenly tracks personal accomplishments.
2. When the Holy Spirit takes full control of our lives, He replaces self-centeredness with Christ-centeredness.

II. Holiness Gives Us a New Level of Spiritual Sensitivity

A. This new spiritual sensitivity helps us recognize temptation, faults, and sin for what they really are.

B. Temptation is simply Satan offering suggestions for us to fulfill legitimate needs in ungodly ways.

III. Holiness Encourages Us to Seek Every Opportunity to Serve God

A. The holy life brings a life of service.

B. We offer our service as a thanksgiving offering to God for all He has done for us.

C. We serve because He first served us.

IV. Holiness Strengthens Our Resolve to Resist the World's Attempt to Squeeze Us into Its Mold

A. It's not an accident that we're picking up stray signals from our culture calling us to conform. God knows all about the world's plan to squeeze us into certain molds.

B. Jesus urged us in John 17 to be in the world but not of it.

We do have to live here, but we don't think and act like the world.

C. The more we're attracted to Christ, the less we're attracted to the world.

Conclusion

The Holy Spirit will help us decide what is crucial to our spiritual growth. We cannot spend a lot of time on the trivial choices. The truth is that the more we are attracted to Christ, the less we are attracted to the world.

THE MARKS OF HOLINESS, PART THREE

Introduction

Jesus said, "Blessed are those who hunger and thirst for righteousness, for they will be filled" (Matt. 5:6). The filling creates a deeper hunger and thirst for more of God than we presently know. Again consider the marks of the Spirit as we see this truth at work in the believer.

I. Holiness Brings Our Greatest Fulfillment in Life from Finding and Doing God's Will

The committed Christian who spends every day immersed in pleasing God finds fulfillment beyond description.

1. As George W. Truett reminds us, "To know the will of God is the greatest knowledge, to find the will of God is the greatest discovery, and to do the will of God is the greatest achievement."*
2. In the end, we're much happier doing God's will than our own.

II. Holiness Gives Us a Hunger for More of God's Presence and Influence in Our Lives

An amazing paradox emerges when believers' lives are totally dedicated to God.

1. We are full and yet seeking to be filled at the same time.
2. We are satisfied and yet hungry, because while God totally fulfills and satisfies us, He also urges us to seek a deeper relationship with Him.
3. Jesus said, "Blessed are those who hunger and thirst for righteousness, for they will be filled" (Matt. 5:6).
4. We find the hunger of our hearts filled with His completeness.

---

*Billy Hughey and Joyce Hughey, *A Rainbow of Hope* (El Reno, Okla.: Rainbow Studies, 1994), 61.

III. Holiness Produces the Fruit of the Spirit in Us

A. God's desired fruit in our lives includes "love, joy, peace, patience, kindness, goodness, faithfulness, gentleness, and self-control" (Gal. 5:22-23). These qualities are in short supply in society. God counts on us to raise a bumper crop of this fruit in our world.

B. As God's Holy Spirit fills us, we produce His fruit naturally as a result of living daily in God's presence.

IV. Holiness Makes Christ the Centerpiece of Life

A. The Father gave us a full-color picture of himself in His Son, Jesus Christ.

B. Everything Jesus said and did in His earthly ministry reflected God's perfect plan, His original intention for all humanity. That's what the writer to the Hebrews had in mind when he said, "Let us fix our eyes on Jesus, the author and perfecter of our faith" (Heb. 12:2).

C. Holiness is about a lot of things, but holiness is more about Christlikeness than anything else.

Conclusion

"Let us fix our eyes on Jesus, the author and perfecter of our faith, who for the joy set before him endured the cross, scorning its shame, and sat down at the right hand of the throne of God" (Heb. 12:2). That is the challenge of the life of holiness.

We don't have the strength and ability to do it ourselves. Rather we fix our eyes on Jesus and depend on His Holy Spirit to work in our lives. Each day we seek to "walk as Jesus did" (1 John 2:6).

The Way of Holiness

Isaiah 35:8-10

Introduction

The prophet Isaiah gives us a glorious picture of what God's grace can do for a sinner. He gives us a standard for life. He shows us that God has set forth a way in which the Christian is to walk. Several characteristics of this life of victory are seen in this prophetic picture.

I. It Shall Be Called "the Way of Holiness" (v. 8)

II. It Is the Way of Purity (v. 8)

"The unclean will not journey on it."

III. It Is the Way of Simplicity (v. 8)

"It will be for those who walk in that Way; wicked fools will not go about on it."

IV. It Is the Way of Safety (v. 9)

"No lion will be there, nor will any ferocious beast get up on it; they will not be found there."

V. It Is the Way of Fellowship (v. 9)

"But only the redeemed will walk there."

VI. It Is the Way of Gladness (v. 10)

"Gladness and joy will overtake them, and sorrow and sighing will flee away."

VII. It Is the Way That Leads Home to Heaven "and the Ransomed of the Lord Will Return" (v. 10)

"They will enter Zion with singing; everlasting joy will crown their heads."

Conclusion

Is it possible in a wicked world to walk on this way? Enoch found this holy way and "walked with God 300 years" (Gen. 5:22). Abraham, Joseph, Samuel, and many other Old Testament saints walked in this holy way. In the New Testament we read of Zechariah and Elizabeth. "Both of them were upright in the sight of God, observing all the Lord's commandments and regulations blamelessly" (Luke 1:6). Then it must be possible under the full light of the Holy Spirit's dispensation of grace to walk with God in this holy way.